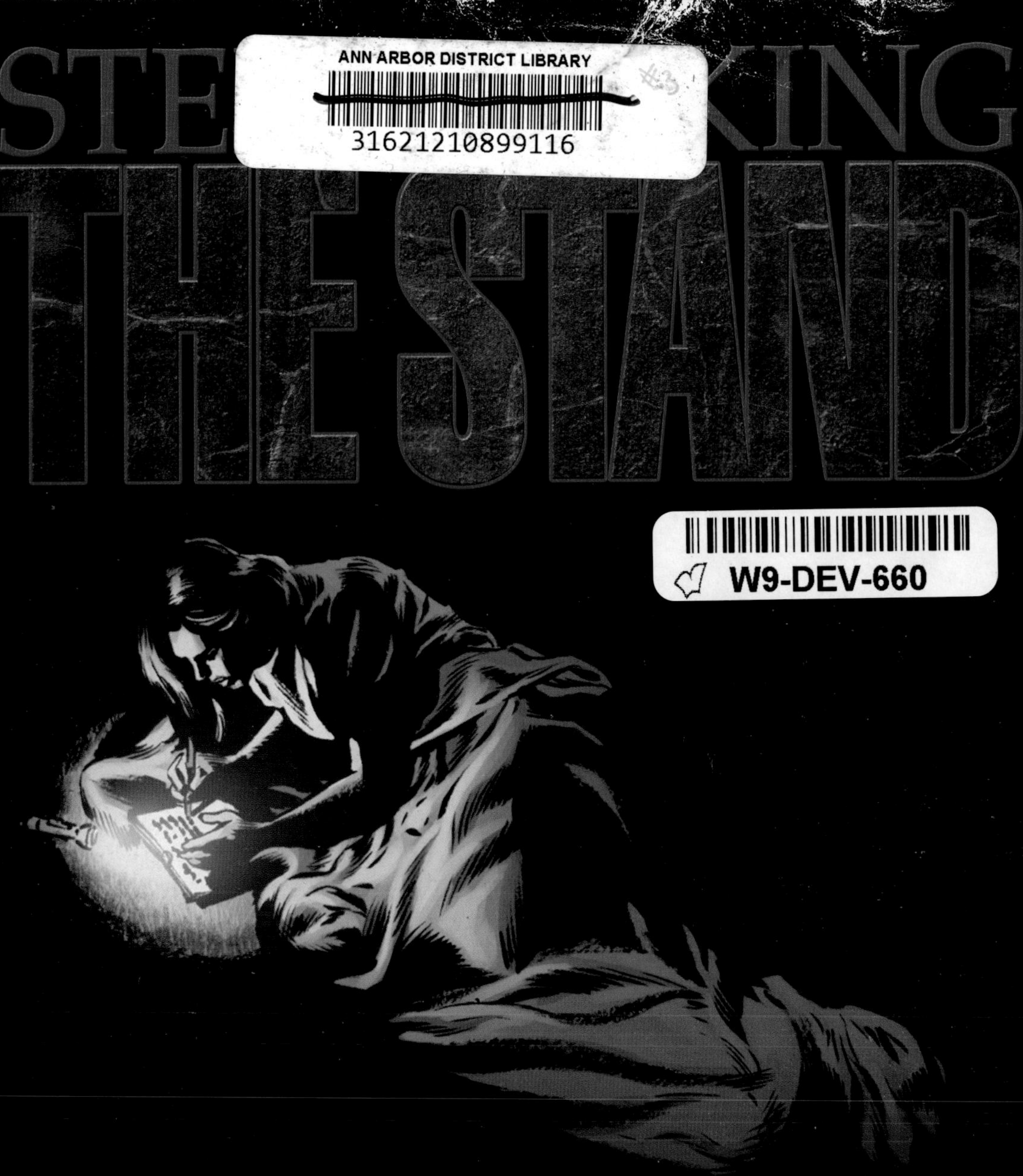

Soul Survivors

THE STAND VOL. 3: SOUL SURVIVORS. Contains material originally published in magazine form as THE STAND: SOUL SURVIVORS #1-5. First printing 2012. ISBN# 978-0-7851-3523-4. Published by MARVEL WORLDWIDE, INC., a subsidiary of MARVEL ENTERTAINMENT, LLC. OFFICE OF PUBLICATION: 135 West 50th Street, New York, NY 10020. $19.99 per copy in the U.S. and $21.99 in Canada (GST #R127032852); Canadian Agreement #40668537. **Printed in the U.S.A.** ALAN FINE, EVP - Office of the President, Marvel Worldwide, Inc. and EVP & CMO Marvel Characters B.V.; DAN BUCKLEY, Publisher & President - Print, Animation & Digital Divisions; JOE QUESADA, Chief Creative Officer; TOM BREVOORT, SVP of Publishing; DAVID BOGART, SVP of Operations & Procurement, Publishing; RUWAN JAYATILLEKE, SVP & Associate Publisher, Publishing; C.B. CEBULSKI, SVP of Creator & Content Development; DAVID GABRIEL, SVP of Publishing Sales & Circulation; MICHAEL PASCIULLO, SVP of Brand Planning & Communications; JIM O'KEEFE, VP of Operations & Logistics; DAN CARR, Executive Director of Publishing Technology; SUSAN CRESPI, Editorial Operations Manager; ALEX MORALES, Publishing Operations Manager; STAN LEE, Chairman Emeritus. For information regarding advertising in Marvel Comics or on Marvel.com, please contact John Dokes, SVP Integrated Sales and Marketing, at jdokes@marvel.com. For Marvel subscription inquiries, please call 800-217-9158. **Manufactured between 4/25/2012 and 5/14/2012 by R.R. DONNELLEY, INC., SALEM, VA, USA.**

10 9 8 7 6 5 4 3 2 1

STEPHEN KING

THE STAND

Soul Survivors

Creative Director and Executive Director
STEPHEN KING

Script
ROBERTO AGUIRRE-SACASA

Art
MIKE PERKINS

Color Art
LAURA MARTIN

Lettering
VC'S RUS WOOTON

Assistant Editors
MICHAEL HORWITZ & CHARLIE BECKERMAN

Consulting Editor
MICHAEL HORWITZ & BILL ROSEMANN

Senior Editor
RALPH MACCHIO

Cover Art
LEE BERMEJO & LAURA MARTIN

Variant Cover Art
MIKE PERKINS & LAURA MARTIN

Collection Editor
MARK D. BEAZLEY

Assistant Editors
NELSON RIBEIRO & ALEX STARBUCK

Editor, Special Projects
JENNIFER GRÜNWALD

Senior Editor, Special Projects
JEFF YOUNGQUIST

Senior Vice President of Publishing Sales
DAVID GABRIEL

Associate Publisher & Senior Vice President, Print Animation & Digital Media
RUWAN JAYATILLEKE

Book Designer
SPRING HOTELING

Editor in Chief
AXEL ALONSO

Chief Creative Officer
JOE QUESADA

Publisher
DAN BUCKLEY

Special Thanks to Chuck Verrill, Marsha DeFilippo, Brian Stark, Jim Nausedas, Jim McCann, Arune Singh, Bill Rosemann, Lauren Sankovitch, & Jeff Suter

INTRODUCTION

And in the end, all they had was their faith. It's no accident that we've titled this segment, midway through our STAND adaptation: Soul Survivors. Our cast is moving past the point where their primary concern is basic survival. Larry, Fran, Nick and the rest are about to become proactive. They're going to join with each other and, as a group, face the awful power of the Dark Man, the Walkin' Dude. This creature of unspeakable evil has infested their dreams; brought them at times almost to the brink of despair. Now, collectively, they're going to take a stand. They will face him down, confront him and demand his departure from this world. Powerful aspirations. Yet, the Walkin Dude is a force to be reckoned with. His powers are unearthly, their source unknown. It's going to take extraordinary courage and unshakeable will to bring him down. Most importantly, it's going to take one more thing: Faith.

These people will have to believe in something larger than themselves if they are to succeed. They will have to possess the absolute belief that they are on the side of the angels and it is their destiny to triumph. And for that they will need a rallying point, a person to lead them who is the stark opposite of the Dark Man.

In the aged Mother Abagail, they have found just such a champion. She is one of King's more fascinating creations. This frail, ancient African-American woman is the center around which the soul survivors will cluster. Abagail Freemantle is a woman of great Christian faith. Yet, she has her moments of doubt. She, too, has sensed the presence of the Walkin' Dude and it has shaken her to the core. But Abagail possesses a spine of steel and a deep belief in the Lord's way. We are all His instruments and we have our roles to play in His Great Design. She is strengthened by these beliefs and by the adversity she overcame throughout her life because of her racial origin. Still, she seems like such a slim reed to hold onto in the coming storm, such an unlikely savior of the remnants of the human race. Her age and delicate physical condition make us wonder if she is up to the task. And the forces in opposition seem so overwhelming.

Prepare now to resume the harsh journey towards salvation or Armageddon. It is at this critical juncture that mankind's future is to be determined. The series of stories collectrf in this volume are a key point in the STAND narrative. While the power of the Dark Man and his minions cannot be denied, never forget that for those who oppose him, unyielding faith can move mountains.

Ralph Macchio
May 2010

PREVIOUSLY

Someone at the Project Blue government facility made a mistake. And now, the deadly flu-like virus "Captain Trips" has killed off 99% of the country's population.

The survivors are tasked with living in a world they no longer understand - and making sense of the evil, faceless man that stalks them in their nightmares.

Among these haunted souls is Nick Andros, a deaf-mute wanderer. Wracked with fever, Nick's visions of the dread Randall Flagg gave way to those of the oldest woman in America: Mother Abagail, who beckoned him to come to her with the promise of sanctuary from Flagg's poisonous influence.

Now, for the first time in his life, Nick makes his way towards a greater destination: A shack in a cornfield in Nebraska...

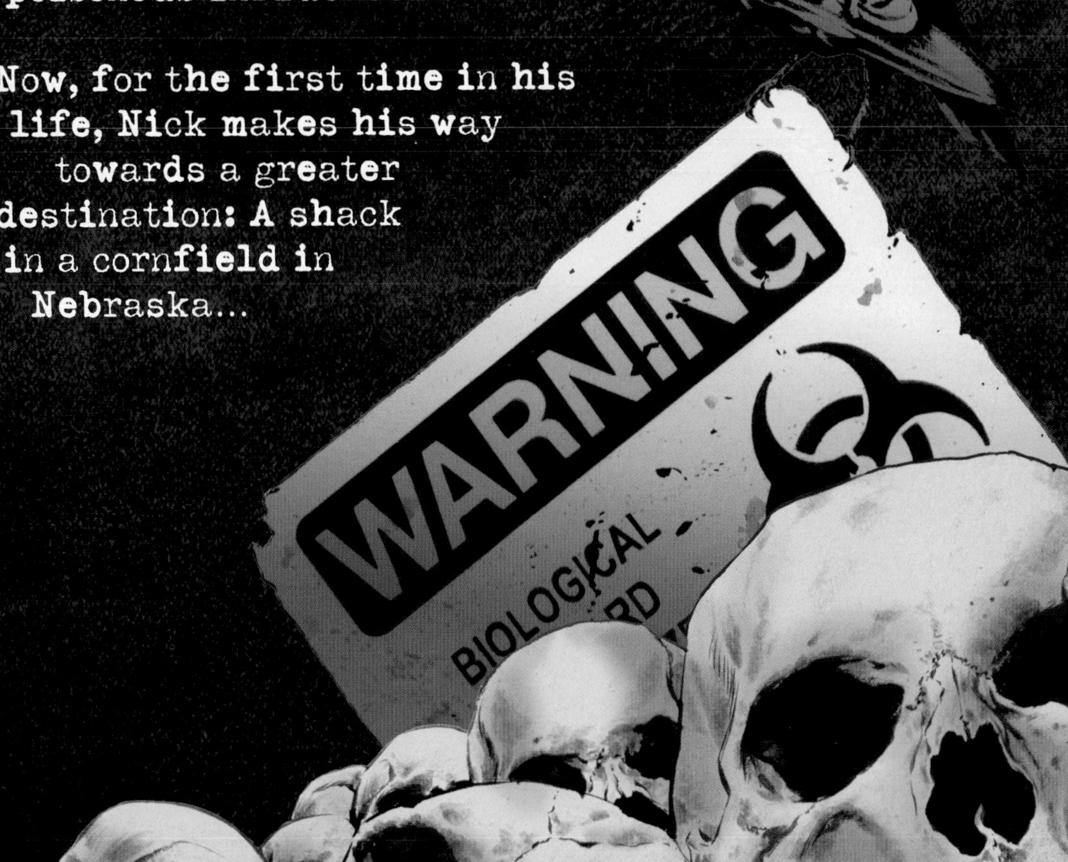

chapter ONE

MAY, OKLAHOMA.
JACKSON'S JU
EVERYTHING MUST GO
SALE
Biking across the country, towards the woman in his dreams, Nick Andros had grown accustomed to seeing dead bodies.
What surprised him, then, was when a corpse sat up in the middle of Route 3 and waved hello.
Hi there, mister!
Nick cut his hands and split open his forehead.
And now the corpse (not a corpse) was talking to him.
Holy gee, mister, but you took a tumble. Didn't you just? My laws!
YOU SCARED ME. THOUGHT YOU WERE DEAD. I'M OKAY. BUT IS THERE A DRUGSTORE IN TOWN?

SALE 40%
EVERYTH MUS GO
I'm Tom Cullen. I can't read. I only got to third grade and my daddy made me quit 'cause I was too big.

Retarded, Nick thought. Great, HE can't read and I can't talk.

Nick tried his best...

...went through his standard dumbshow...

...but it was no use.

Got a toothache? Is that why you don't feel like talking?

Anyway, Nick had already spotted what he was looking for:
A drugstore.

DRESS
FOR THE SUMMER
Hey, mister, you can't do that! That's illegal!
M-O-O-N spells il-*legal.* Don't you--
AAACHOO!
GET YOUR FLU SHOT!
KE-R-RASH!!
What are you, anyway, deaf? My laws! Are you...
While Nick looked for peroxide, Tom had one of his "episodes."
(Blackouts that were, in fact, instances of almost "normal" thinking.)
My laws! You're deaf 'n' dumb, right? Can't hear! Can't talk! Right?
I thought of it! Hooray for me! ***Hooray for Tom Cullen!***

They got to know each other over lunch, in the town square across from the courthouse.
Afterwards, Nick wondered about May's total emptiness.
He gestured to the large circle of buildings that made up its downtown.

Again, Tom had an episode, and Nick worried his new friend was dying.

But then he jerked out of it, as if the word EUREKA had appeared over his head.
You want to know where all the people went!
Well, I guess they went to Kansas City. My laws, yes. Just like my daddy, he run off with a waitress, her name was M-O-O-N, that spells DeeDee Packalotte--

Tom launched into a monologue, and Nick thought:
A deaf-mute and a man who's mentally retarded... Of what possible use could we be to each other?

One night, Nick reasoned. I'll stay one night, then leave him in the morning.

THE NEXT DAY.
Nick found Tom playing with a fleet of toy Corgi cars and a plastic Texaco station...

...and was suddenly swept by a totally unexpected sadness. A feeling so deep he feared he might weep.
I can't. I can't leave him.

You moving on, mister?
Nick nodded--
--then pointed to himself, to Tom, to his bike, to the road that led out of May.

Want me to go with you?

Laws, yes! Tom Cullen's going! Tom Cullen's--
--can I take my garage?
TEXACO

Tom **loved** the bicycle Nick found for him, **loved** the basket for his garage, **loved** the Klaxon horn Nick had added on a whim--
Wistfully, Nick wished he could hear it, to see if it pleased him as much as it seemed to please Tom.

They rode north on Route 23 for two hours, trying to outrace the thunderclouds encroaching from the west.

At the outskirts of Rosston, the sky turned a still, ominous yellow. Nick felt nervous, without knowing why.

(He'd never learned that one of the few instincts man shares with animals is exactly that response to a radical drop in air pressure.)

Tornado! There's a tornado coming!

While Nick looked for a funnel, Tom raced away, into the field off the road, beating a twisted path through the high grass--

Damn fool, Nick thought, He's going to snap his axle!

Nick pedaled to beat the devil, to catch Tom before he vanished into the decaying structure, but--

No go.
And from the way Tom had tossed his bike aside, there was no question: he was scared out of his skin.

Nick risked one last look over his shoulder--

A horrible darkness was coming out of the west. Not a cloud, more a...total absence of light. Nick thought:
I am looking at whatever is in my worst dreams, and it is not a man at all, although it sometimes LOOKS like a man. What it really is, is one almighty big black twister sucking up everything unlucky enough to be in its--

Quick! Quick! Oh my laws, yes!

In the last instant of light, Nick saw they were sharing the storm cellar with a family of rat-gnawed corpses--

Then came the **slam** Nick didn't hear--

--and then they were in perfect darkness, while the tornado's mad, thrumming vibrations intensified above them.

Nick felt Tom shaking against him and wondered if he was crying. Even the **air** seemed to be trembling against Nick's face.

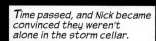

Time passed, and Nick became convinced they weren't alone in the storm cellar.

And it wasn't the corpses. Nick felt the presence of...

The dark man, the man who came to life in his dreams, the creature whose spirit he had sensed in the black heart of the cyclone...

Nick's panic rose, he was about to lunge for the stairs--

--when a flood of dazzling light blinded him.
It was Tom, who'd left his side and opened the door at the top of the stairs.

When his eyes readjusted, Nick scanned the cellar--
If there was anyone else down there with him, Nick didn't see him. (Nor did he want to.)

Nick's watch insisted that he and Tom had only spent fifteen minutes in the storm cellar.
Never before had Nick understood how subjective, how plastic, time really is.
He would've guessed an hour, maybe two.

Once topside, Nick realized why the light had been so blinding.
The barn's roof and walls had been torn off, leaving behind something that suggested the skeleton of a prehistoric monster.

Tom had righted the bicycles--
(A miracle they were still there, thought Nick, and a testament to the tornado's fickleness--)
He was standing with them, shivering and crying.

He saved my life, Nick thought. I'd never seen a twister before in my life. If I'd left him behind in May, I'd be dead as a doornail right now.

Someone was down there with us. Someone who came out of the twister.
Can we go now? Please?

JULY 7th.
NEAR THE OKLAHOMA-KANSAS BORDER.
YOU ARE LEAVING
HARPER COUNTY
OKLAHOMA
YOU ARE ENTERING
WOODS COUNTY
OKLAHOMA

You know what, mister? I've never been out of Harper County, laws no, but I know this sign. My Daddy showed it to me once.
Is it the *world?* Is *Woods* the word for *world,* I mean. Are we going into the world, mister?

Nick nodded, and they started pedaling.
And he thought: It IS the world, and the world is EMPTY. It's not just Shoyo or Texarkana, it's AMERICA, lying like a huge discarded tin with a few forgotten peas rolling around in it.

KANSAS.
THAT NIGHT.
While Tom slept, Nick studied an atlas and realized...
There really **was** a Polk County, Nebraska, like from his dreams.
Did that mean they were actually gonna find an old black woman sitting on her porch with a guitar, surrounded by corn?

That night, Nick dreamed of the man with no face--and then of corn higher than his head--and of the sound of music...

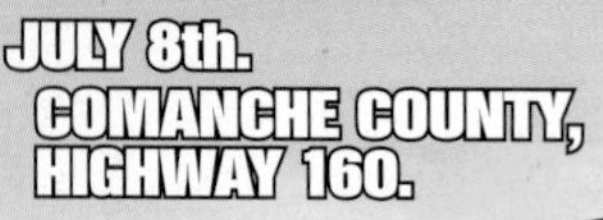
JULY 8th.
COMANCHE COUNTY, HIGHWAY 160.

What are they? Those ain't cows!

JULY 10th.
Another scorcher.
Also, the day they passed an apple tree and ate its small, sour fruit.
Nick stopped after two, but Tom ate six, greedily.

That made him sick, of course, and Tom couldn't ride his bike anymore.

CORBETT'S
CORBETT
DRUG ST
When they reached the town of Pratt, at 4:00 in the afternoon, Nick called it quits for the day.

In the drugstore, looking for some Pepto-Bismol for Tom, Nick saw a mannequin out of the corner of his eye.
Only it wasn't a mannequin, it was Julie Lawry.
Jesus, are you real? Or a ghost?
Why ain't you saying anything?
Nick went through his dumb show again (with quicker results this time).
You can't talk? You're a mute?
Well, you ain't bad-looking. That's something.
Nick could smell at least three different kinds of perfume on her.
My name's Julie, Julie Lawry. What's yours?
You can't tell me, can you? Poor you.
I'M NICK. I'M TRAVELLING WITH TOM CULLEN, WHO IS LIGHTLY RETARDED. WE'RE GOING TO NEBRASKA. COME WITH US, IF YOU WANT.
Okay.
I'm so glad to see someone, who cares if it's a retard and a deaf-mute?

My mom and dad died two weeks ago. Everyone died but me. I've been so *lonely...*
You *are* sort of cute...
Hey, let's make it!
I can't believe this, Nick thought...
...but it was real enough.

LATER.
Is that the retard?
TEXACO

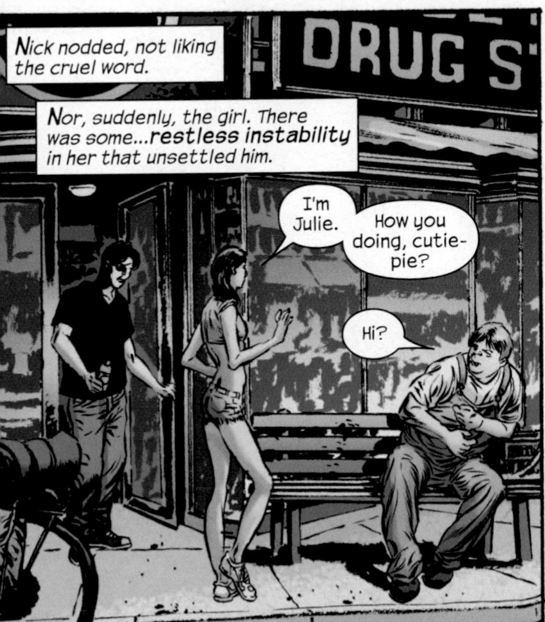
DRUG S
Nick nodded, not liking the cruel word.
Nor, suddenly, the girl. There was some...**restless instability** in her that unsettled him.
I'm Julie.
How you doing, cutie-pie?
Hi?

Uh-uh. I ain't gonna.
Tom Cullen don't like medicine. Laws no, tastes bad.

That's right, Tom. Don't drink it, it's poison.
PEOPLE'S STORE
AZCO INVESTM
F

Tom Cullen doesn't drink poison! Daddy said if it'll kill the rats in the barn, it'll kill Tom! No poison!

SLAPP!

LAWS!

You...
You dummy freak bastard! It was just a joke! You can't hit me!
As Nick wrote his note, he thought: Of all possible people, why her?

WE DON'T NEED YOU!

What? No. No, I'm coming with you--
--and you can't stop me.

But, in fact, he could.

She looked different. Somehow **real** for the first time.
A gun was something she **couldn't** manipulate to her own advantage.
I...I didn't mean it.
I'll do anything you want, honest.

STORE
INVESTMENTS
Feeling soiled and depressed, Nick kept the gun on Julie until she vanished around a corner, two blocks away.

When he turned back...
...Tom was nowhere to be seen.

Great.
Thanks a lot, Julie.

TWENTY MINUTES LATER.
Nick found Tom a few blocks away from Pratt's business district.
Please don't make me drink it, laws no, Daddy says if it'll kill rats, it'll kill me... pleeease!
211

But Nick had given up on that idea.
Let the gunk in Tom's stomach run its course, however long it takes.

I'm sorry, Tom Cullen's sorry...

They walked back to Main Street together--

Julie, Nick thought--

--as he felt something whiz by, grazing his face.
Tom shrieked and took off; Nick turned around--
Just in time to catch the muzzleflash of **another** blast in a window of the Pratt Hotel--
Julie, Nick thought again, taking off after Tom--
PEOPLE STORE
That night, they slept in a barn three miles north of Pratt. Miraculously, none of Julie's shots had landed, however many times she tried.
Nick's last conscious thought was, **Well, at least we're done with that hellion...**
...though that would turn out to be only **half**-true.

JULY 12TH.
They were riding bikes they'd acquired in Iuka when, at a quarter to three in the afternoon, Nick saw something in his rearview mirror.
A twinkle of something.
A good old Detroit Chevy truck, rolling along US 281.
Nick felt a stab of panic in his heart.
What if it was Julie driving that truck? What if she still had her gun?
It wasn't, thank God.
Holy cripes on a carousel, am I glad to see you boys! Climb on up here and let's see where we're going.
And that, friends, was how Nick Andros and Tom Cullen met Ralph Brentner.

chapter TWO

SOMEWHERE IN NEW ENGLAND.
Larry Underwood was cracking up.
He walked all day long, every day, from sunrise to sunset.
(After Rita and after his wipe-out, he hadn't been able to ride his motorcycle anymore.)
He was suffering from malnutrition, heat prostration, and plain old exhaustion.
The last week, he'd been unable to sleep because of the nightmares.
About Rita.
About the Dark Man.
Come on, Larry, we'll get it togeeeeether, Laaarry--
Daytimes, the vision of the Dark Man would recede. Daytimes, it was the Big Alone that went to work on him.
NOW ENTERING
MAINE
VACATIONLAND

Though...was he alone? Throughout his journeys, he had a strong feeling of "watched-ness."
If someone's there, why don't you come out? I won't hurt you.
But nothing.

Maine saved his life. He found a house in the shade of a tree where there was food and water, and it was cooler.
He ate--cleaned himself up--and slept, dreamlessly.

And realized: Just because he wasn't up for a motorcycle, it didn't mean he had to walk.
For the first time in a long time, he laughed aloud. (Even though it was at his own stupidity at not having thought of a bicycle sooner.)

In North Berwick, he stopped being afraid of whoever was following him. He just wanted to see somebody again. Anybody.
To your health!
9
10
Wells
Sanford

In Wells, Larry flipped a coin and turned south on US 1.
And two miles down the road saw it for the first time. This huge, blue animal, lazy and slow.

It was the end of the East.
The place where the sea takes over.
Land's end.

He'd never seen so many birds in one place before.
The thought formed before Larry could push it away: Gulls are carrion-eaters. The pickings must be real good just lately.
He stood in awe for a half-hour. An hour.
I'm here, he thought.
Larry felt...overcome. Cleaned out and fresh.
At first, he thought the scream was coming from the gulls--
But it was behind him--
AIIEEEEE!
JOE!!

Larry thought: He's come to kill me. This boy...
...what did I ever do to him?
He reacted without thinking--
(Larry felt instant pity. The kid looked fierce, but there was nothing to him.)
Don't hurt him! He's only a little boy!
Let go of the sticker, kid.
Keeping his foot on the boy's wrist was like standing on a wounded, vicious snake.

Let...it...
go, Joe.

Let it
go...
...or
I'll leave
you.

She spoke calmly,
persuasively.
No one would hurt him.
No one would abandon him.
Everyone could be friends...
if he would let go of the
damn knife.

Eventually,
the boy did.

Larry felt the old defensive, self-serving words rise--
I had to do it, it wasn't my fault, lady, he would've killed me--

But he stopped himself. The situation was what the situation was, and it could've ended much worse.
Larry thought: I think I've changed somehow. I don't know how much...
No one can tell what goes on in between the person you were and the person you become. There are no maps of the change. You just...come out the other side.
Or you don't.

I'm Nadine Cross. This is Joe. We're happy to meet you.

Larry Underwood.
You two have been following me.

That was how Larry, Nadine, and Joe met at the end of the world.

WELLS PUBLIC BEACH.
THAT NIGHT.
"I want us to come with you, Larry, wherever you're going. I guess there's no way to be coy about it, under the circumstances..."

That boy... worries me, Nadine.
His knife's gone... but the world's full of knives, lying around, waiting to be picked up.

Nadine explained how she came across the boy in Epsom, sick on the lawn of a house from some animal bite, and nursed him back to health.
At first, she tried dressing Joe (which is the name she gave him), but he tore off everything except for his underpants.
He never talks, just growls and grunts.
Feral as he is, she's been able to control him--mostly.

I don't want to sound brutal...

...but would you consider leaving him behind?

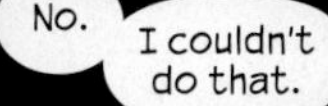
No.
I couldn't do that.

Nadine was thinking that this man was a link in a chain she had been following for years, a chain that was now nearing its end.
I understand the danger, but...
If I left him, that would be the same as murder. I won't be a party to that. Too many have died to kill more.
I'll be responsible for his actions.
The surf rolled and boomed as Larry deliberated.
How much had he changed?
...
I think you're being dangerously softhearted, but... all right.
And hopefully Joe won't cut my throat in the middle of the night.
A sudden certainty that her words about the sanctity of life would someday soon rise up and mock her swept Nadine like a cold wind. She shuddered and thought: No, I'll not kill. Not that. Not ever.
To change the subject, she asked about the guitar Larry had found in a house up the shore, along with the food they'd just eaten.
Do you play?
Yeah, I do.
Let's see what we've got here...

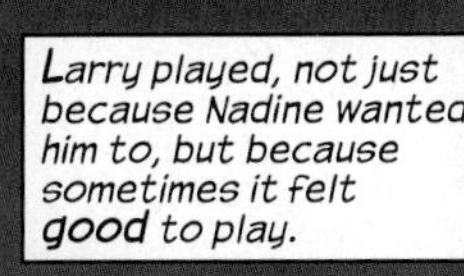
Larry played, not just because Nadine wanted him to, but because sometimes it felt good to play.

Especially when you were on a beach, at night, with a bonfire and a pretty woman.
It was a beautiful guitar, and it made a beautiful sound.
Larry sang an old blues song he had learned as a teenager, and when he finished--

Look--

Music hath charms...

Larry played more--
Folk, and blues, and primitive rock and roll--
He played until his fingers failed him--

At which point:
It takes a lot of practice...

Larry shrugged inside.
He'll probably smash it to hell...
No, I don't think so.

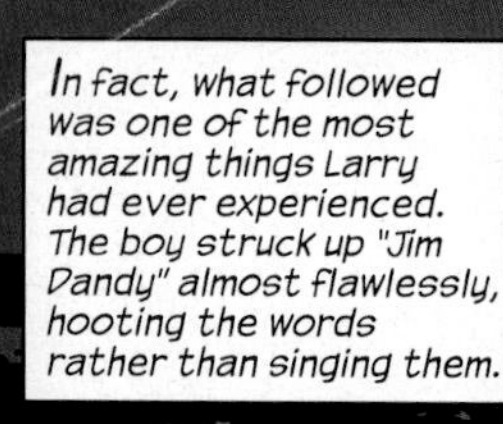

In fact, what followed was one of the most amazing things Larry had ever experienced. The boy struck up "Jim Dandy" almost flawlessly, hooting the words rather than singing them.

At the same time, both he and Nadine knew: Joe had never played a guitar before in his life. He was copying Larry. Like some kind of...prodigy.

But he wasn't bearing down on the strings hard enough. And his chord changes were sloppy.
Here, let me show you--

All right. All yours.
When you want a lesson, I'm here.

That night, Joe slept with his arms wrapped around the guitar he'd adopted.

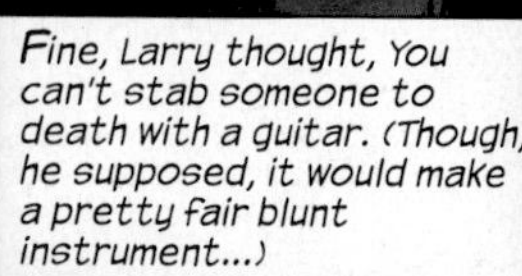

Fine, Larry thought, You can't stab someone to death with a guitar. (Though, he supposed, it would make a pretty fair blunt instrument...)

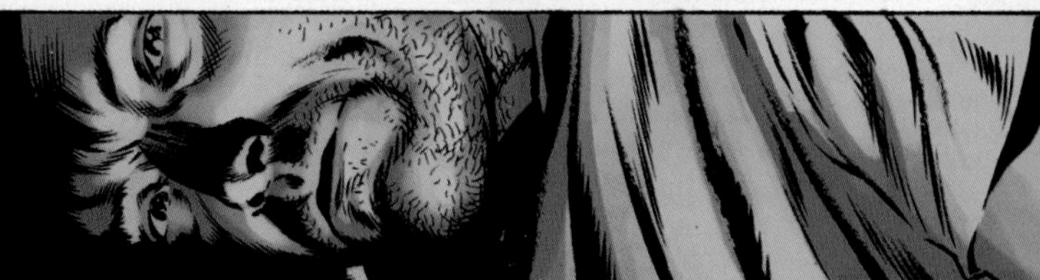

The next morning, Joe played Larry's own song "Sally's Fresno Blues," and Nadine made oatmeal and hot tea for breakfast.

Larry's spirits buoyed.
Nadine was a beautiful woman, after all, and as for the boy...
...well, you couldn't **not** like someone who liked the guitar as much as Joe did.

They cycled along Route US 1, Joe leading the way, sometimes as far ahead of them as a mile.
At eleven o'clock, Larry and Nadine reached Ogunquit.
Why would they have blocked the road?
They must have tried to quarantine their town.
I bet we'll find another roadblock on the other end.

What they found, first, was the essence of honky-tonk beach resort. Summer cottages, clam shacks, gas stations, and Dairy Queens, all jammed together.
YUM · YUM
FRIES
SEA FOOD
Not very pretty, is it?
No, but it was ours, once.
Now it's gone.

They caught up to Joe a little further along, pointing at something, just off the highway.

US 1 TO WELLS 95 TO PORTLAN
LEAVING OGUN. JULY 2
The plague center...
Why didn't I think of that?
Nadine...

...can you drive?
A motorbike?
I think so.

What Larry was suggesting dried the moisture in his mouth and made his temples pound, but if they were going to catch this Harold and Frances...
We'd have to be very, *very* careful...
And take it very, *very* slow, at first.

While Nadine made lunch, Larry explored the barn.

And found something carved in one of its support beams that...stirred an excitement in his stomach.
Good for you, Harold...

After lunch, he and Nadine went to a Honda dealership in Wells, and from the way the bikes were lined up, Larry deduced that two of them were missing.
Harold and Frances strike again.

He also found a crumpled chocolate bar wrapper on the floor, nearby.
Which one had aimed for the wastebasket and missed?
Probably lovesick Harold...

That night, Larry lay in his blankets wondering if Nadine would come to him. (He **wanted** her, and thought she wanted him, too.) But she didn't. At least not before he fell asleep.

Larry dreamed:
He, Joe, and Nadine were following the sound of someone playing a guitar through a field of corn...

...to a shack and an old woman who made him feel good. The way his mother had, when he was a little boy.
Well say, I got me comp'ny. Come on closer so's I can see you.

Larry felt they were in a kind of forever place, where the sun seemed to stand still, one hour from darkness.
He wished they could stay. The man with no face couldn't get them in this place.

Boy, you like to have a swing on this old box o' mine?

Bless 'im, he plays good. Me, I'm too old now. It's the rheumatiz. But in 1902 I played the County Hall.
Who are you?
Mother Abigail is what they call me and I still make my own biscuits. You come see me as quick as you can. We got to go before he gets wind of us.
Before *who* gets wind of us?
A cloud passed over the sun--
The tire swing stopped its gentle arc--
Joe quit his playing--
The black man. The servant of the Devil. We got the Rockies between him 'n us for now, praise God, but we got to knit together. In Colorado. God showed me where.
But we got to be as quick as we can. So you come see me in Nebraska. There's others coming, too.
No. We're going to Vermont--that's *all.*
To. Vermont.
There was pity in Mother Abigail's face--and anger in her voice.
You'll go straight to Hell, Daughter of Eve, if you don't mind yourself. And when you get there, you're gonna find that Hell is *cold*--

That was the end of Larry's dream, which burned away with the morning fog before they set off for the Plague Center.
Slow, remember. We're not going to hurry and have an accident.
I'm just excited. It's like being on a quest.

Larry couldn't help but think that Rita Blakemoor had said something very much like that when they left New York...
...two days before she died.

ENFIELD, MAINE.
A TWENTY-MINUTE REST BREAK.
Nadine... what did you do before?
First and second grade teacher. A private school in Pittsfield.
I loved the little ones. The little ones are the only good human beings.

That explained her complete unwillingness to leave Joe behind.
Were you married? Before?

No, never married.
I'm the original old-maid school teacher, younger than I look but older than I feel. Thirty-seven. My hair's premature.

Nadine...

I wish you wouldn't.

You don't want me to?
No. I don't.

*But...she **did** want him to, that was the thing. Larry could feel the want coming off her in waves.*
Nadine--
Lady--

Lady--
Oh, thank heaven--

Oh, my God, are you *really* people?

Yes, we are.
And *that* was how Larry and Nadine found out Joe could talk, and how they met Lucy Swann.

QUECHEE, OVER THE STATE LINE IN VERMONT.
THAT NIGHT.

Lucy's story was simple and not much different from their own or the others they would hear.

Her people got sick. Her husband, her daughter. They died. She buried them.

She thought she might go mad from the loneliness and the senselessness of it all, especially when the dreams started.

Dreams?

Nightmares. Mostly it's a man chasing me, but I can never see his face exactly because he's wearing a cloak and stays in the shadows. They got so bad I was afraid to--
Brrr-ack man!

Brr-ack man! Chases me! Bad dreams! Brr-ack man dreams!
This is crazy, Larry thought, we're all having--

Lucy, do you ever dream... about a place in Nebraska?
I had one dream about an old black woman... She said something like, "Come see me..."

Joe, do you ever dream about, uh, corn? An old woman? A little house with a porch?
Leave him alone, Larry, you'll upset him.

A swing, Joe? Made out of a tire?

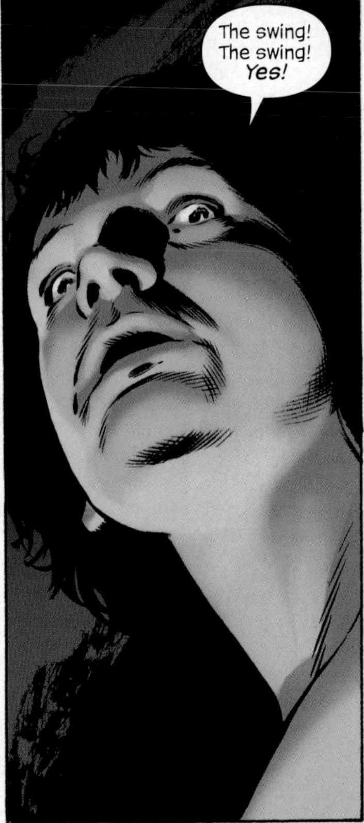
The swing! The swing! Yes!

We're all having the same--
Wait, why are we all having the same dream?

Have you had them, too, Nadine?
I don't dream.

Larry thought: **You're lying. But why?**
Nadine, if you're--

That closed the matter.

*And that night, while the foursome slept, Larry dreamed of the Dark Man. He was coming for him, through the corn, and he **wasn't** empty-handed...*

JULY 19.
AFTER BIKING ALL DAY.
Oh, God.
Oh, no...

THE STOVINGTON PLAGUE CENTER.
route 7 to Rutland. route 4 to Schuylerville route 29 to 1.87 1.87 South to 1.90 1.90 west
C.D.C
everyone dead. going to Nebraska follow our route watch for signs H.L + F.G + Stu Redman + Glen Pequod Bateman JULY 8

Harold, my man, can't wait to shake your hand and buy you a Payday.
Larry--

Larry looked down.
For whatever reason, dreams or no dreams, Nadine had fainted dead away.

chapter THREE

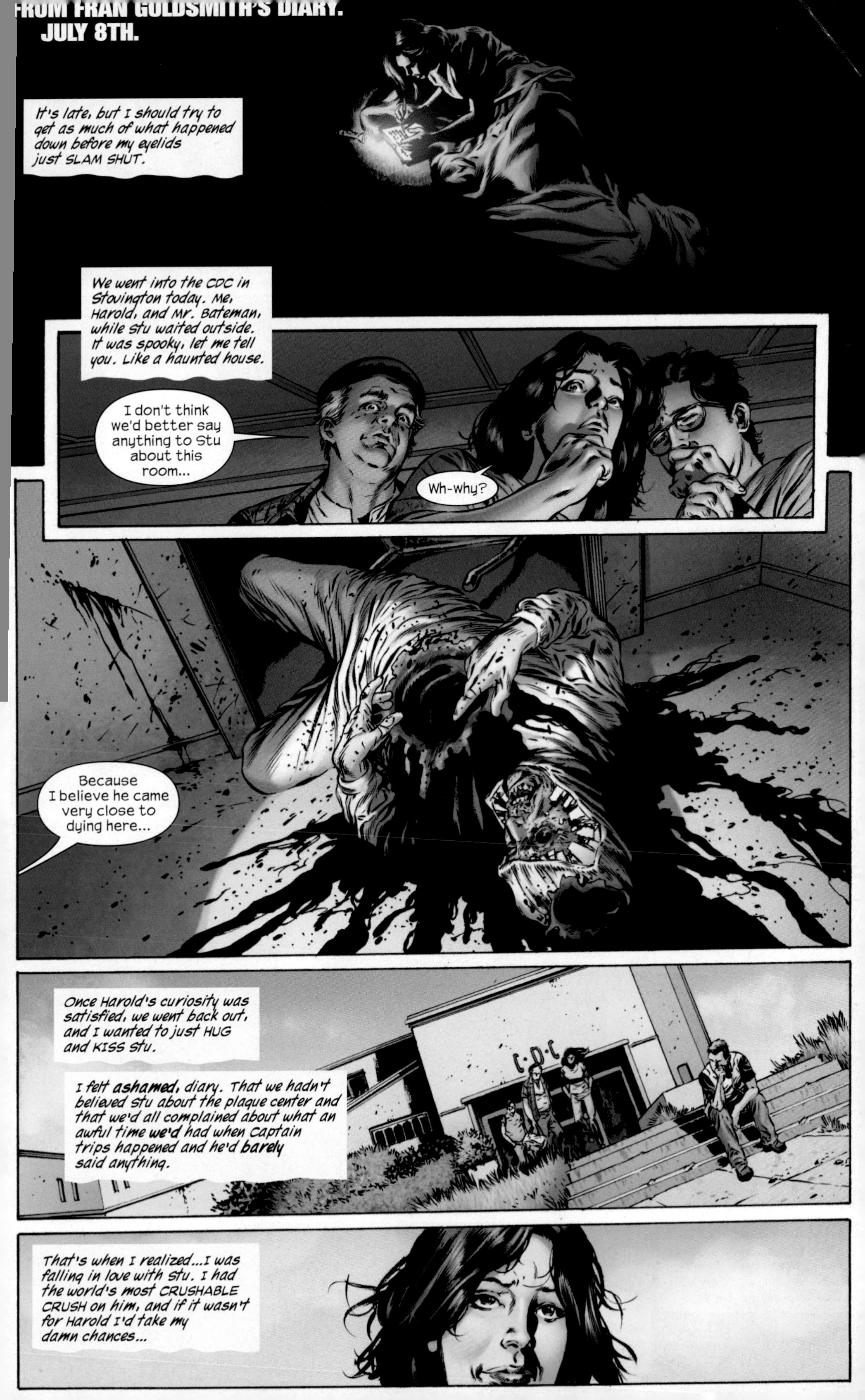

FROM FRAN GOLDSMITH'S DIARY.
JULY 8TH.

It's late, but I should try to get as much of what happened down before my eyelids just SLAM SHUT.

We went into the CDC in Stovington today. Me, Harold, and Mr. Bateman, while Stu waited outside. It was spooky, let me tell you. Like a haunted house.

I don't think we'd better say anything to Stu about this room...

Wh-why?

Because I believe he came very close to dying here...

Once Harold's curiosity was satisfied, we went back out, and I wanted to just HUG and KISS Stu.

I felt **ashamed,** diary. That we hadn't believed Stu about the plaque center and that we'd all complained about what an awful time **we'd** had when Captain Trips happened and he'd **barely** said anything.

C·D·C

That's when I realized...I was falling in love with Stu. I had the world's most CRUSHABLE CRUSH on him, and if it wasn't for Harold I'd take my damn chances...

Anyway, that was when Stu told us he wanted to go to Nebraska.

He wanted to check on this old lady he'd been dreaming about lately, he said.

Her name's Mother Abagail, I think, and she lives in a place called Holland Home or Hometown or something like that. In a field of corn.

While Harold made his sign, we had a very sober talk about our dreams.

Dreams we'd each been having, in some shape or other. About this woman. And about a bogeyman with no face.

It's remarkable...

...but we all seem to be sharing an authentic *psychic* ***experience.***

Once we'd settled on a plan to find Mother Abagail (I'd take ***her*** over the Dark Man anytime), Harold suggested we stock up on veronal and start taking small doses.

To disrupt these dream-cycles.

To stop the nightmares from coming.

I plan to palm my dose because I don't know what they might do to the Lone Ranger inside me.
Besides, bad as the Dark Man is, I like seeing Mother Abagail in my dreams. She so exudes an aura of NICENESS and KINDNESS.

I understand why Stu wants to go to her. I keep thinking if we can just get to her, everything will be A-OK.

Things to Remember, diary: The Who. Kool-Aid. Converse All-Stars. **Night of the Living Dead. Brrrr!** That last one hits too close to home. I quit for the night!

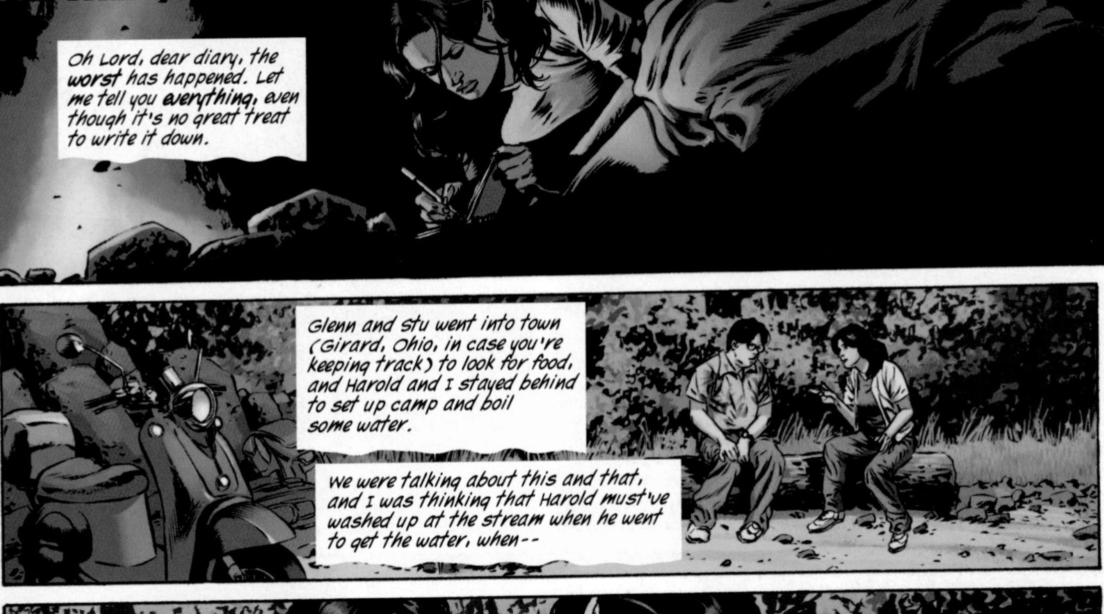
JULY 14TH.
Oh Lord, dear diary, the worst has happened. Let me tell you everything, even though it's no great treat to write it down.

Glenn and Stu went into town (Girard, Ohio, in case you're keeping track) to look for food, and Harold and I stayed behind to set up camp and boil some water.
We were talking about this and that, and I was thinking that Harold must've washed up at the stream when he went to get the water, when--
Harold!

I was so surprised, I fell right off the log. And Harold found it necessary to say:
Are you all right, baby?

And then it all came out. The bad dreams, the worrying about the baby, my feelings for Stu, the traveling, the stiffness, everything...
...and I started GIGGLING.

Followed by hysterical laughter.
What's so funny?
I giggled and laughed and sobbed until Harold must've thought I'd gone absolutely bonkers.

After a bit, I managed to pull myself together.
Fran, I find this difficult to say...
Then maybe you shouldn't.
The giggles almost came back, then, but I bit down on my tongue.

Frannie... I love you.

I guess I knew all along it was just as bald as that.
I don't love you, Harold.

...
It's him, isn't it? It's Stu.

I...don't know.

I know, all right.
Even though he said he didn't want you! That you could be mine!

Now I have a temper I can't always control--a gift from my mother--and I could **feel** it starting to strain its leash.

Just like giving you a new pair of shoes, huh?

No one **OWNS** me, Harold.

I've **met** guys like him before, Frannie.

He's the quarterback who throws spitballs at you when you're reading your composition aloud 'cause it's the best in the class. The guy who goes steady with the cheerleader and thinks he's number one with a bullet.

Yeah... good luck with **that.**

Then he just walked off, and it was like he'd had some secret dream and I'd just shot it full of holes.

Honest to gosh, I felt terrible for him, diary, because he wasn't **playing** hurt, he **WAS** hurt. And whipped.

But what Harold has to see is that his head has got to CHANGE first. He's GOT to see the world is going to stay the same as long as HE does.

Anyway, I'm sure Harold's onna be watching Stu and me o see what happens next.

Oh, it makes me sick and pointlessly angry to write that.

What **right** does he have to watch us? What right to complicate this miserable situation we're in?

Things to Remember: The Texas Rangers had a pitcher named Nolan Ryan. There were TV comedies with laugh-tracks. You used to be able to get frozen cakes at supermarkets. Sara Lee were my favorites.

JULY 30TH.
Oh, diary. It all happened so fast and was so horrible, but let me see if I can write it down in some kind of sense.
Our caravan was heading towards Indiana, when we swept around a curve and came face to face with a blockade.
I quickly counted twelve people: Four men and eight women.
I stopped so suddenly, I almost skidded out.
You all right, Frannie?
Dismount.
All of you.
Whoever he was, diary, he made me time-travel inside my head to when that state trooper pulled me over for speeding.
I wondered if he was gonna ask to see our drivers' licenses next.
Dismount, dammit. NOW.
That's when I thought: "We're sitting ducks."
And it struck me how odd it was:

Four men...eight women....

Four men!
Eight women!

Stu--
Harold, don't--
That's when all hell broke loose.

Don't you try it, fat boy--
Garvey, Virge, Ronnie--kill them but save the woman!
I realized, in that moment, that we were probably all gonna die there.

But then one of the women screamed:
NOW!
KENT STATE

What happened next took seven seconds.
One:
Glen was stunned, not moving. Harold was pulling on his guns, forgetting they were in their holsters. Stu's rifle was in his hands suddenly. Mine, too.
Two:
The bearded man, who had been aiming at Stu, turned around and shot (and missed) the blonde woman.
(I screamed Stu's name anyway, diary.)
Three:
Stu was on the ground, up on both elbows, firing.
Four:
Five:
One of the other men shot one of the other women point-blank in the face.
I closed my eyes, but I swear I actually heard her blood raining down on the pavement like from a storm.
Six:
The olive-skinned man shot at me.
Seven:
Harold fired at the olive-skinned man.

Both shots missed.
I was trying to fire my gun, to kill the olive man before he killed Stu (Stu!) or Harold or me, but it wouldn't fire.
That's when Stu got him.
It was like Bonnie and Clyde, diary, there was blood EVERYWHERE!
Meanwhile, the blonde woman (who were these people?) was struggling with one of the men for his rifle--
--while three of her companions fought for possession of the third man's shotgun.
Glenn sat in the road, as if he didn't know where he was or what was going on, exactly.
CHAOS.
INSANITY.

Once the second man got his rifle back, I thought he would shoot the blonde woman. Instead, he wheeled on the three women huddled against the Country Squire.
Yaaa! Die, you &*(^%$#! Yaahh! Die!!
One woman went down; the other two ran.
Stu fired at the shooter and missed--
Come on!
--even as the second man gunned down one of the running women.
Harold and Stu fired at the shooter at the same time.
Both hit their target.

The third man--the only man still alive--staggered from the carnage...
...the woman in the Kent State sweatshirt hot on his heels, wailing on him.
KER-RUNCHH!
Then there was silence.
Then the fluttering of a bird taking flight.
Then the Kent State woman let out a long, primal scream...
...that I know will haunt me for the rest of my life.

We were all in shock after it happened.
The NINE of us, now.
The blonde woman was Dayna Jurgens, from Xenia, Ohio.
The girl in the Kent State sweatshirt was Susan Stern.
The one who had squeezed Shotgun's crotch was Patty Kroger.
The eldest woman was Shirley Hammet.
No one knew the last woman's name; no one had ever heard her talk.
Glenn was holding my hand, muttering:
You mustn't let it affect you. Such horrors...bound to occur. Best protection is in numbers. Society, you know. Society is the key...
Yes, Glenn.
The grass was still wet from the previous night's rain.
White butterflies, sluggish because their wings were heavy with moisture, circled around us...

We walked until we found a farmhouse, diary. Just off the highway, west of Columbia, over the Indiana state line.

Dayna did most of the talking.

She had left Xenia in the company of two men, she said, Richard Darliss and Damon Bracknell.

Around the 8th of July, they all started dreaming about a boogeyman. A "hardcase" who was getting an army of "hardcases together" so he could enslave all the other survivors.
(And let me tell you: That chilled me, diary.)
In Williamstown, they came across an overturned dump truck in the highway.
That's where Danya and her companions had been ambushed by the four "hardcases." They executed Richard and Damon and took Dayna prisoner.
I was the fourth addition to their "harem," they called it.
Or sometimes "zoo."
The hardcases had been in the army, apparently. They were moving across the country, killing any men they met and capturing the women so they could rape them over and over.
Doc, the leader, was very taken with you, Fran. I could tell.
The men kept the women sedated on pills. Uppers in the morning, downers at night.
The last couple of days, though, they'd been palming the pills. Which is why they'd been able to fight back this morning.

Still, it wouldn't have worked if you hadn't gotten wise, big fella.
I didn't get wise soon enough, looks like.
Next time, I will.
Stu looked at Dayna, then, really looked at her for the first time, and I admit it...I felt jealous.

She was pretty, despite everything. And I doubt she's pregnant.

"Oh, my God," I thought, "I went and did it! I waited too long!"

And maybe I'm crazy, but I believe Harold saw the same thing between Stu and Dayna, and I swear--I swear--he was smiling in relief.

Ugh, that's all I can write down at this point, diary, while everyone else is asleep or at least pretending to sleep.
Oh! Except that no matter what happens between Stu and Dayna, I will never be with Harold. Never-EVER-Harold.

Things to remember:
I'm sorry, it must be my state of mind, but I can't remember a thing!

JULY 31ST.

Where to begin, diary?

Harold and Glenn had gone into Brighton to find a CB radio, Dayna and the women were back at camp, and I was looking for Stu, who had gone off by himself.

Hello?

I found him, smoking a cigar that made me think of my father's pipe.

Frannie, want to share my rock and watch the sun go down?

Oh, boy, did I ever.

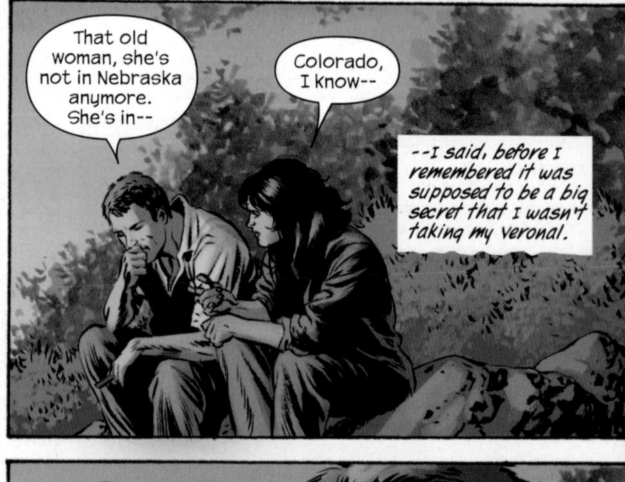

That old woman, she's not in Nebraska anymore. She's in--
Colorado, I know--
--I said, before I remembered it was supposed to be a big secret that I wasn't taking my veronal.

...
You're not the only one. I talked to Dayna, and she and Susan aren't taking it, either. And I'm not.
We were all feeling...out of touch.

In my dreams, Mother Abagail's sitting in a pickup truck on Highway 76 and she's telling me to move it along faster.
There's...lots of people with that old woman now.
In *my* dreams.
The other people still alive...they're going to her.
Or to the other one.
The Dark Man.
Yeah, I've been dreaming about him, too. He's setting up somewhere in the desert. Las Vegas, maybe. And Frannie...
"That's what I dreamed. Dayna, too. Crosses along Highway 15 made out of telephone poles. People hanging off them."
...I think he's *crucifying* the people who give him trouble.
He's doing *what?*
That's just--
--just a dream.
But I didn't believe the words even as I said them. There WAS a madman or a demon or whatever out there, crucifying people.

Frannie, why did you stop taking the Veronal?
Oh, there's...
...there's no counting on what a woman will do.

I suppose not, but there are ways to find out what they're thinking, maybe.
What--?

He kissed me, diary, and then we made love, and then--

--and then we lay in the grass, holding each other, as it got darker and darker around us.
I've wanted you for a pretty long time now.
Me, too. But...
I don't want trouble with Harold.

He's got the makings of a fine man if he'll toughen up.
There's also...
The real reason I stopped taking the pills...
I thought they might be bad for the baby.

For the--
You're pregnant?
And no one but you knows, not even Harold!
I thought he would either leave immediately (like Jess would've, if he'd found out I was pregnant with another man's child) or he would hug me.
But all he did was LOOK at me, diary, for a long time.
And I couldn't help it, I kept thinking of Daddy and when I told him in the garden.
When are you due?
January--
--I said, the tears coming.
And he didn't say that I shouldn't worry or that he would take care of everything, but he made me feel that way, diary, by the way he held me and made love to me again.
And I knew Stu and I were TOGETHER now, and that the others would find out soon--about us, about the baby--but right now, it was our secret.
And that until we get to Mother Abagail and the others, Harold CAN'T SUSPECT A THING. (Sounds like a line from an old Bette Davis movie, doesn't it?)
More later--I need my rest tonight, no matter what dreams may come.
LATER. PAST MIDNIGHT.
Frannie slept heavily and dreamlessly that night.
So did they all, in fact--

--except for Harold Lauder.
Who looked down at Frannie and thought: We're in the dog days of summer now...
Every dog has his day.

He took Fran's journal back to his sleeping bag and read everything.

It's late, but I should try to get as much down before my eyelids just SLAM SHUT...
He felt like the little boy he'd been, with few friends and many enemies. The boy who had turned to books--to reading--for solace.
He read everything about Frannie and her love for Stu.

He read and remembered his fantasies about all the pretty girls at Ogunquit High. How they would please him and he would chastise them with small leather whips.
Frannie had been one of those girls.
Every doggy has his day...

In the hour before dawn, he replaced the diary in Frannie's pack. He wasn't careful about it, thinking if she woke, he would kill her and then run.
But not to Colorado or Nebraska...

...to the desert.
Harold crawled into his sleeping bag, and when sleep came, it was thin.

He dreamed he was dying, somewhere in the desert.
High above him, cruising buzzards rode the night thermals, eager to make a meal of him.
Then a frightful, vulpine red eye opened in the dark and looked at him.
And beckoned him.
To the west, where shadows were even now gathering, in their twilight dance of death...

THE NEXT DAY.
Harold smiled all day long.

He smiled even though they didn't make it across Indiana as quickly as they hoped, hitting a horrible clog of army vehicles near the Elkhart interchange.

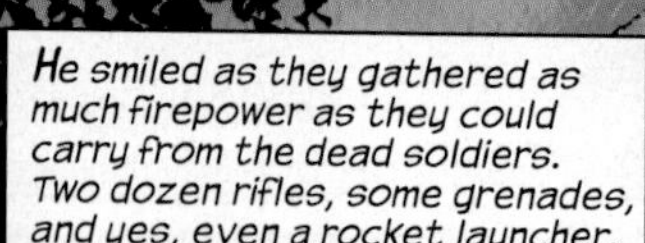
He smiled as they gathered as much firepower as they could carry from the dead soldiers. Two dozen rifles, some grenades, and yes, even a rocket launcher.

He smiled as he and Stu struggled to figure out the rocket launcher, for which there were, count 'em, seventeen rockets.
Don't blow yourselves up, for God's sake.

He smiled so much that when the group started bunking down for the night, Frannie remarked:
You know, Harold, I don't think I've ever seen you feeling so good. What is it?

He winked at her and said something puzzling.
Every dog has his day, Fran...
That night, Harold began keeping his own journal.

chapter

FOUR

JULY 20th.
HEMMINGFORD HOME, NEBRASKA.

At twenty to eleven, Mother Abagail emerged, with toast and coffee, as she did every day that her Coca-Cola thermometer read over fifty degrees.
It was the finest summer she could recollect since 1955; pity more folks weren't around to enjoy it.
Though, this day and age, did they ever?

She supposed young people in love did, reveling in themselves and in warm July nights, and old folks whose bones remembered the death-clutch of winter, but...

...most everyone was gone now.
God had brought a harsh judgment down on the human race, one **some** people might condemn Him for, but not Mother Abagail.

After all, He had done it before with water, and further along, He would do it with fire, she supposed, and anyway, it wasn't **her** place to judge God.
On such matters, she was satisfied with the answer God gave Moses when he asked the burning bush, **Who are you?**
I Am, Who I AM.
In other words, Moses, stop beating around this here bush and get your old butt in gear...
Mother Abagail laughed and dipped her toast into the coffee until it was soft.
She'd lost her last tooth sixteen years ago. Toothless she had come from her mother's womb, toothless she would go into her grave...
In the meantime, she wished she could sit and enjoy the cycles of the seasons. She **hated** that she had to be a part of what was coming next, but what do you get when you question God?
I Am, What I AM.
Even when His own Son prayed that the cup be taken from His lips, God never answered... and she wasn't anywhere **near** up to that snuff, no way, no how.
Just an ordinary sinner was all she was, and it frightened her to think God had looked down at her in 1882 and decided:
I got to keep her around a goodish time. She's got important work on the other side of a whole heap of calendar pages.

Her final season of work lay ahead of her in the West, near the Rockies.
And what did God care how miserably afraid Abby Freemantle was of the man with no face, he who stalked her dreams?
She never saw him; she didn't have to see him.
He was a cold pocket of air...
...a shadow passing through the corn at noon...
...a gore-crow peering down from a phone line.
Sometimes, when she heard the nightwind in the corn, the Dark Man seemed only a little less powerful than God Himself...
Like the dark angel that had flown over Egypt, killing the firstborn of every house where the doorpost wasn't daubed with blood...
Welladay.
God is great. Thank You for the sunshine, and for the coffee, and for the fine BM I had last night, You was right, those dates turned the trick...
Mother Abagail turned her face up to the warm sun and dozed.
And her heart, its walls now as thin as tissue paper, beat on and on...

Things had surely changed since the Freemantles had come to Nebraska as freed slaves.
Her father, John, had bought the land a smidge at a time. He'd been the first man in Polk County to try chemical fertilizer, to try crop rotation...
...and, in March of 1902, Gary Sites had come to the house to tell him he'd been the first black man in Nebraska voted into the Grange.
At twenty years of age, Abby thought she was the only one in her family (other than her daddy) who understood what a truly unprecedented thing that was.
As unprecedented as when she was asked, later that year, to play her guitar at the Grange Hall, in the white folks' talent show.
What?!
You and Sites and Frank Fenner whipped this idea up, John Freemantle, and that's fine for them, but they're white!
You talk about plowin' with 'em, and go downtown and have a beer with them, that's fine, but this is different! This is your daughter!
What are you gonna do if she gets up there and they laughs at her or throw rotten tomatas at her? What are you gonna say when she asks why you let them do that to her?
Well, Rebecca, I guess we better leave it up to Abby and David.

David Trotts had been her first husband. A quiet, thoughtful farmhand from over Valpariso way.
Whatever Abagail thinks is right, why...I reckon that's what to do.
So on December 27, 1902, Abagail Freemantle Trotts, three months pregnant, stood on the Grange Hall stage in dead silence after the master of ceremonies announced her name.
Every chair was taken, plus stand-room-only.
The hall was a sea of white faces.
Including that awful Ben Conveigh, who hated her father and made nasty cracks like saying that when black babies go to heaven and get their little black wings, you call 'em bats instead of angels.
To the side, pressed against the wall, under the kerosene lanterns, were her mother, father and husband.

Her heart was thudding in her chest, and she was thinking: I promised Daddy I wouldn't cry no matter what, but Mama was right, I've got above my place--
Then she stilled herself and thought:
I'm Abagail Freemantle Trotts, I play and sing well; I do not know these things because anyone told me.
And so she began to sing "The Old Rugged Cross."
Hymns led into a medley of Civil War songs, and the audience started to sway and tap their knees, almost in spite of themselves.
"When Johnny Comes Marching Home," "Marching through Georgia," "Goober Peas," ending with "Tenting Tonight on the Old Campground."
There. Now if you wanna throw your tomatas, you go ahead. I sang my best and I was real fine.
But their applause was full and sustained. Her mother was weeping, her father and husband beaming. Cries of "Encore! Encore!" filled the hall.

Thank you all very much. I'll sing one more song...
"...the best song I know on account of what President Lincoln and this country did for me and mine, even before I was born, making it possible now for my family to be living with the fine neighbors we have."
Then she played and sang "The Star-Spangled Banner," and everyone stood up and listened and some cried--
--and when she finished, the crowd applauded fit to raise the roof.
That was the proudest day of her life.
Yessir, 1902 had been a topper of a--
Welladay!
She awoke from her nap a little after noon.
Time to make her way to the privy her grandson Victor had put behind the house in 1931.

Year before last, her great-granddaughter Molly and her husband Jim had wanted to put in a proper flushing toilet, but some things you couldn't let go.
And she'd had a feeling at their suggestion.

As if God had spoken to her the way he had to Noah:

Abby, you are going to need your hand-pump. Enjoy your 'lectricity, but keep your oil-lamps full and the wicks trimmed. Keep your cold-pantry stocked. And mind you don't let the young folks talk you into anything against My will. They are your kin, but I am your Father...

She finished making water, poured lime down the hole, and came out into the yard.

The corn was going to be fine this year...

Sad and bitter for her to think that she wouldn't be at Hemmingford House to see summer give way to pagan, jocund autumn.

Please my Lord, my Lord, not unless I have to, take this cup from my lips if You can...

No answer but the creak of the rope from the tire swing and the crows off in the corn.

That night, she dreamed she was a young girl again, about to make her Grange Hall debut.
I am Abagail Freemantle Trotts, and I play and sing well; I do not know these things because anyone told me.
She began to play "Rock of Ages," thinking:
With the help of God, I am going to win them over. I will make David and Mamma and Daddy proud of me, and I will bring music from the air and water from the rock and--
--and that's when she saw him, far back in the corner, and the words dried up in her mouth.

God?
Lord?
What's that coon doing up on our stage? No coon ever brought music from the air! No coon ever brought water from the rock!
All hell broke out, then.
She saw someone punch her husband in the mouth--
Someone else wrestling her mother down to the ground--
A third man kicking her father--
MOMMA!
And the force of her cry seemed to break the room apart--

Then she was her too-old self again, in the mystic corn behind her farm, and she wasn't alone...
He spoke with the soft voice of doom:
I have your blood in my fists, Old Mother. If you pray to God, pray He takes you before you ever hear my feet coming up your steps. It was not you who brought music from the air, not you who brought water from the rock...
...your blood is in my fists.
She woke up the hour before dawn, covered in a night sweat as heavy as May dew.
My Lord, my Lord, take this cup from my lips...

That morning, she set off for Addie Richardson's farm and henhouse, four or five miles away.
She was going to have company soon, and dreams or not, tired or not, she had never been one to slight company and she didn't intend to start now.
FREEMANTLE
HEMMINGFORD HOUSE
Her hope was to reach the Richardson farm by noon, sleep through the hottest part of the day, kill her chickens, then come home in the gloaming.
She wouldn't get back to Hemmingford House until after dark, and that made her think of her dream from the night before, but **that** man was still far away and--
My company's closer.
She fell to thinking about her past again.
She'd had five children by David. One of them, Maybelle, had choked to death on a piece of apple in the backyard of the Old Place.
The only one of her children to die an accidental death.
David died in 1913, of an influenza not so very different from the one she'd just survived.

Her second husband, Henry Hardesty, a farmer from up north, died when his tractor turned turtle on him in 1925.
A year later, she'd married Nate Brooks, one of Henry's hired men, and oh, how people had talked.
But Nate had been a good man, who had pretty much done as she'd told him.
Her six boys had produced thirty-two grandchildren, who had produced ninety-one great-grandchildren, that she knew of, and--at the time the superflu hit--three great-great-grandchildren.
She had outlived them all, and that was not the way it should be, but...the Lord had His plans.
Which is why she said what she said when she turned a hundred and they sent a TV reporter to do a story on her.
To what do you attribute your great age?
To God.
Welladay and hallelujah.

She reached the Richardson farm completely exhausted, but needed to do one last thing before her nap.

A lot of animals had died with this disease, and she had to know if chickens were among them. (And wouldn't it be a bitter laugh if that **were** *the case?)*

But as she neared the henhouse, she heard the telltale clucking and cackling.
All right. That's good, then.

She came across Bill Richardson's body, well picked over by foraging animals.
Flights of angels sing you to y'rest, Billy Richardson.

Finally, she turned back to the cool, inviting farmhouse, for a rest and some food.
It wasn't far at all, just across the dooryard, but she was so utterly exhausted, she wasn't sure she would make it.
Lord's will be done.

When she next woke up in the guest bedroom, the light was too bright; every muscle and fragile bone in her body was in agony; and she realized, after a moment:

God A'mighty, done slep' the afternoon and the whole night through!

Limping, she went outside, crossed to the henhouse, and slipped inside--

--**wincing** at the hotness and the smell of decomposition. (The weakest birds had starved or been pecked to death).

Then, grunting and puffing, she dragged the three plumpest chickens--along with Billy Richardson's hatchet--to the chopping block in the yard.

Now Lord, I got me three broilers and I should like to whack off their heads and not m'own hand, Thy will be done, amen.

She thought: **The only thing dumber than a broody hen was a New York Democrat--**

THUNNKK

That accomplished, she put the birds into her towsack, hung Billy Richardson's hatchet where she found it, and headed back to the farmhouse to wait out the worst of the day's heat.

She napped during the early part of the afternoon and dreamed that her company was getting closer now.

Six of them, and one was a boy who was deaf and dumb, but a powerful boy, all the same.

He was the one she would have to talk to.

She awoke at three-thirty, plucked the chickens, ate a stale peanut butter sandwich, and gathered herself.

I'm off, Lord. Don't reckon to get home until midnight, but the Book says fear neither the terror of night nor that which flieth at noonday. Walk with me, please. Jesus's sake, amen.

Two miles later, it was full dark, her strength seemed about gone...but she felt strangely exhilarated.
How long had it been since she'd been out after dark, under the canopy of stars?

A warm night like this made her remember her girlhood again, its gorgeous vulnerabilities as it stood on the edge of the Mystery. Oh, she had--

Your blood is in my fists.
A sudden sharp tug at her sack made her heart jump--
Hi!

There it was, between the gravel shoulder and the corn, its eyes picking up glints of moonlight.
Another weasel joined the first.
And another.
And a fourth.
And more.
Until they lined both sides of the road.
They were smelling the chickens in her bag...
How could so many of them have crept around her?
She'd been bitten by a weasel once, when she was twelve.
She'd reached under the porch of the Big House to get a red rubber ball, and the weasel--with what felt like a mouthful of needles--had fastened on to her forearm.
It took her father beating it with a piece of stovewood before the vicious thing let go.
She'd been terrified of the creatures ever since, the way some people were of snakes or spiders, which made her think:
He had sent them--the Dark Man.

One bit at the rough hem of the towsack--
Hi!
Your blood is in my fists.
It was all for nothing. If I don't give them my chickens, they'll rip me to pieces. All for nothing.
In the darkness of her mind, she saw the Dark Man smile, his fists held out, blood dripping from them.
Another tug at the bag.
And another.
The weasels were squirming closer and closer...
But whosoever believeth in Me, behold, he shall not perish...for I have put My sign on him and no thing shall touch him...he is mine, saith the Lord...

Get out!
It's chicken, all right, but it's for my company! Now you all git!

The creatures' eyes filled with unease--
Then drew back, away from her, melting into plumes of smoke--
A miracle, she thought, filled with exultation for the Lord--
--but then, she went cold, suddenly.
Somewhere, far to the west, beyond the Rockies, she felt an Eye open in the sky and turn toward her, searching.
Who's there? Is that you, old woman?
He knows I'm here...
Oh help me, Lord. Help me now, help all of us...
But then the Eye either closed or turned away...
...and Mother Abagail resumed her walk home again.

JULY 24.
She began at seven in the morning with the pies. A blueberry, two strawberry-rhubarb, and an apple.
Just the act of cooking comforted her because cooking was life.

By early afternoon, her kitchen was filled with the smell of frying chicken.
It came out just as light and as nice as you could want.

After putting the chicken on paper towels, she sat on her porch and started playing her favorite hymns.
She was settling down to "We are Marching to Zion" when she heard it.

An old Chevrolet farm truck, coming down the Country Road.

Praise God for bringing 'em through.

My Lord, I thank You so.

Yee-haw! Hi there, Mother!
Nick said he thought you might be here and here you be!
That's him, Mother Abagail thought. The boy who was just finishing up learning about being a man...
Hello, Nick. I'm glad to see you, God bless.
You're all welcome here!
The Lord has brought you and Mother Abagail is going to feed you!
We can't stay long, but before we do any moving on, we'll rest, and break bread together, and have some fellowship...

chapter FIVE

EMMINGFORD HOUSE.
There was little talk during the meal, mostly just grunts of pleasure, then Ralph Bretner declared:
That was one dilly of a meal, ma'am. I can't remember when anything hit the spot so good. Thanks are in order.
Can I come and sit with, grammylady?
Oh, Gina, honey, I think you'd be too heavy.
Nonsense, Olivia. The day I can't take a little one on my lap is the day they wind me in a shroud. Come on over, Gina.
Now tell me what happened to your leg.
I broke it when I fell out of a barn.
Dick fixed it. Ralph says Dick saved my life.

Nick, Tom Cullen, and Ralph happened on Dick Ellis halfway across Kansas.
Dick had been a veterinarian in his previous life.
The next day, passing through Lindsborg, they heard the faintest cries coming from the south side of town.
If the wind had been blowing the other way...
God's mercy.
Gina had been on her own for three weeks when the rotting floorboards in her uncle's barn gave way beneath her.
They found her a day after her fall, and though Dick had been pessimistic about her chances, she bounced back with a speed that surprised them all.
I suspect her condition, when we found her, had as much to do with loneliness as anything else.
'Course it did.
If you'd missed her, she would have just pined away.

: started raining,
o they moved to
he kitchen.

Mother Abagail lit three oil-lamps to push back the dusk.

Maybe the old ways are best.

I only mean... that's the first home-cooked meal I've had since, well, June thirtieth, I guess.

My wife, Helen, now she could... She...

For a moment, they all listened to the rain. Alone, it would have been a desolate sound. In company, it was a secret sound, closing them in together.

Thunder muttered, but far away, back over Iowa.

Gina yawned, her eyes wide and glassy.
That was the cue.
Tom Cullen's tired. M-O-O-N, that spells tired.

Hearty thanks were made again, sleeping arrangements were decided upon, and then it was just the three of them.
Looking at Nick, Mother Abagail felt a quiet sense of knowledge and completion.

At one end of her life, there had been her father, John Freemantle, tall and black and proud...

...at the other end, this man: young, white, and mute, with that one, brilliant expressive eye.

You two are the head ones, I figure, so we got some stuff to sort out.
Not me. I was a full-time factory worker and a part-time farmer. I've raised a helluva lot more calluses than idears in my time. Nick, I guess he's in charge.

Is that right, Nick?

He wrote his answer:
IT WAS MY IDEA TO COM UP THIS YES
ABOUT IN CHARGE I DON'T KNOW.

Have you seen other folks on your travels?
We've heard things, like motorcycles. And it feels like we've been watched. So there are other people around. We think what scares them away is seeing a fairly big group all together.

Why did you come here?

I DREAMED OF YOU. DICK, TOO. THE LITTLE GIRL DESCRIBED THIS PLACE - THE TIRE SWING

Bless the child.
What about you, Ralph?
Once or twice, ma'am. Mostly, I dreamed about... that other fella.

She thought of squirming weasels. She thought of the red eye, searching not just for her now, but for a whole party of men and women... and one little girl.
What other fella?

DARK MAN

INTERLUDE.
It isn't-- the flu, is it, Harold?
Is it food poisoning?
No, it's nothing like the flu.
None of us know, Fran, Glen thinks it might be Mark's appendix.
PERION McCARTHY AND MARK BRADDOCK.
Lovers who'd joined their party a few days before.
You've got to help him, Glen. You've got to do something. You can't let him die.
If it keeps hurting as bad as this...I'd rather be dead...
We gave him some aspirin, Dayna, for what it's worth.
Hopefully it's his bowels. Too much roughage.
He wouldn't be running a fever if it was his bowels. And his belly wouldn't be swollen that way.
Fran felt dread rise in her like a black column. There wasn't a doctor or nurse among them, and if it was Mark's appendix...
What are we going to do?
She was thinking of her baby now: What if it has to be a cesarean birth?
Maybe, if it is his appendix, we ought to try...well, operating on him.

It's his appendix, no doubt about it.
But we'd kill him if we tried to operate on him ourselves. You know that, Harold.
He'll die if we don't *try.*

Even if we could open him up without having him bleed to death, we wouldn't know his appendix from his pancreas. Not to mention, what would we use?
The nearest hospital is back in...Maumee.

We move him, his appendix bursts and dumps enough poison into his system to kill ten men.
But Harold's right. If we don't do anything, he'll die.

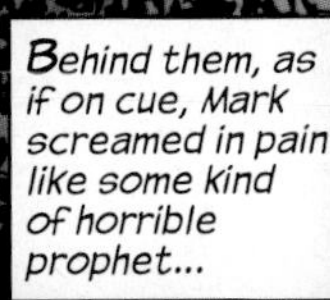
Behind them, as if on cue, Mark screamed in pain like some kind of horrible prophet...

It shouldn't be like this...
Having your appendix out is supposed to be nothing!
Maybe in the old days... but it's *something* now.

HEMMINGFORD HOUSE.
I've been told, in a dream, by the Lord God...

...that we're to go west.
I didn't want to listen. This piece of land's been my family's freehold for a hundred and twelve years, and all I want to do is die here, but that's not meant to be.

I started having dreams two years before this plague fell on us. I've always dreamed, and sometimes my dreams have come true...

Prophecy is the gift of God and everyone has a smidge of it...

My own grandmother used to call it the shining lamp of God, sometimes just *the shine...*

"In my dreams, I saw myself going west until I could see the Rocky Mountains. With just a few people at first, then a whole caravan, two hundred or more. And we could see signs, road signs..."

Boulder
CITY LIMIT
ELEV 5363 FT

I always felt someone special would come to me, and that's how I'd be in the way of knowing the time to move had come, and...

...it's *you,* Nick. God has put his finger on *your* heart.

I DON'T KNOW ABOUT GOD, BUT SOMETHING IS WORKING HERE. HAVE YOU DREAMED ABOUT ANY OF THE OTHERS? GINA?

Not any of the ones who came with you, but...

"A man who doesn't talk much... A young woman who is with child... A man who comes to me with a guitar of his own."

HOW MUCH DO YOU KNOW ABOUT THE DARK MAN?

He ain't Satan, but he and Satan have kept their councils together of old...
"He's the purest evil left in the world...
"The rest of the bad is *little* evil. Shoplifters and sexfiends and people who like to use their fists. But he'll call them. He's already started. He's getting them together a lot faster than we are...
"Not just the evil ones, but the weak ones, the lonely ones...the ones that have let God out of their hearts..."
MAYBE HE'S NOT REAL. MAYBE HE'S JUST... THE BAD, SCARED PART OF US ALL !!!

You dreamed of me, and ain't *I* real? And I dreamed of you. And praise God, you're sitting right there.
He's as real as you or I.
"The Bible don't say what appened to Noah's family after the flood went down. But I wouldn't be surprised if there was some awful tussle for the souls of those people.
"And I wouldn't be surprised if that's what was in store for us..."
He's west of the Rockies now. Sooner or later he'll come east, when he's ready. And it's our lot to deal with him.
Oh, yes. There's bitter days ahead. Death and terror, betrayal and tears.
And not all of us will be alive to see how it ends.
I don't like any of this. Aren't things hard enough without this guy you and Nick are talking about?
It's God's way. He don't explain to the likes of Abby Freemantle.

IF THE DARKMAN IS WEST, MAYBE WE OUGHT TO PICK UP STAKES AND MOVE EAST.

Nick, all things serve the Lord God. Don't you think this Dark Man serves Him, too? Run away, but the Dark Man will follow you. God *wants* you to face him.

I DON'T BELIEVE IN GOD.

Bless you Nick, but that don't matter.
He believes in *you*.

HE NEXT DAY.

How is he, Peri?

Sleeping. The others have gone to Kunkle, to look for a doctor's office, to get some books and... instruments.

We're really sorry...

I guess that doesn't sound like much, but we really are.

I know that. This is no one's fault.

Unless there's a God, of course, then it's *His* fault.

They'd met in Albany, Perion had told Frannie, on the last day of June. Almost immediately, they decided to travel together. She had begun to love him, a little more each day, and now this...

He was good to me, Fran.

So very... very...kind to me.

Perion...

HEMMINGFORD HOUSE.
The day they spent at Abby Freemantle's place was the best any of them could remember since the super-flu had drawn away, like the waters going down from Mount Ararat.
Tom Cullen, for instance, spent the day racing through the corn, scaring up droves of crows.

Gina McCone played with a set of paper dolls Abagail had found in her bedroom closet.

The women, Olivia and June, spent the day in the kitchen, cooking...

...while Mother Abagail took Dick and Ralph to the Stoners' farm to get a pig for supper.
Better let me, boys, she's sure to be a gusher.

Conspicuously absent was Nick, who'd taken off to be by himself.

Abagail knew what the boy was wrestling with, and her heart went out to him...

MEANWHILE.
Stu?

It's here! There's the little bastard, right there!

Fran, show me the other diagram again! Quick! Quick!
Can you take it out, Stu? Sweet Texas, do you think you can?

Stu?

I don't know, Glen, it's self-containing above and below, the appendix, it's--
Wipe my forehead, Fran, I'm sweating like a pig!

Hand me the scissors, Glen! The small pair!
Stuart.
He finally looked at Perion:
You don't need to, anymore. Mark's dead.
He died almost two minutes ago.
You... you're sure?
Thank you...
Thank you all for trying...
For the longest time after the operation, all Stu could say was: "That's that. All over. That's that."

FTER NINE
'CLOCK.
ey were all on the porch,
atting and laughing, when
ck rejoined them.
Conversation broke off, as if they had been marking time, waiting for him.
WE BETTER START FOR BOULDER TOMORROW
I don't want to any more than you do, but I guess we better.
What made up your mind?
Nick pointed at her angrily.
She had made him their leader. Or the others had. Either way, it was like a bad joke and he didn't like it.
It scared him that everything Mother Abagail had said to him might be true.
So be it.
My faith's in the Lord.

DAWN, THE NEXT DAY.
Stu...?

I was dreaming again, about the Dark Man and the old woman...
We were wrong, she's not *in* Colorado, she's getting ready *to go to* Colorado...
Oh, Frannie...

What is it? What's wrong?
I woke up, from the dreams, and...it's Perion.
She got to the Veronal in Glen's pack and... she's dead, Fran.

Lord, what a mess...
I guess I've got to wake the others up and tell them...

When does it end?

I... I don't think it does.

In that moment, what Fran bestowed upon Stu was not a lover's hug.
It was simply one survivor clinging to another...

...though, to Harold, there was no difference whatsoever.

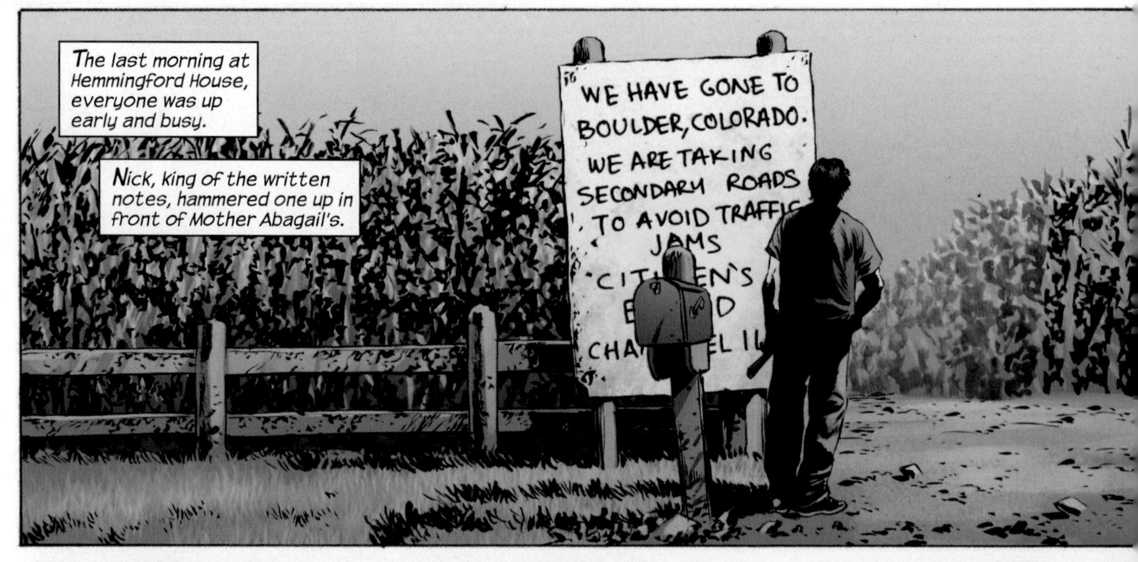
The last morning at Hemmingford House, everyone was up early and busy.
Nick, king of the written notes, hammered one up in front of Mother Abagail's.
WE HAVE GONE TO
BOULDER, COLORADO.
WE ARE TAKING
SECONDARY ROADS
TO AVOID TRAFFIC
JAMS

Do you know, Nick, my daddy once owned all this land for miles around? It's true...
And I played my guitar down at the Grange Hall in nineteen and oh-two. Long ago. Long, long ago...

Oh, Nick, I have harbored hate of the Lord in my heart...

"Abby," the Lord says to me, "There's work for you far up ahead. So I'll let you live, until your flesh is bitter on your bones...

"I'll let you see your daddy's land taken away piece by piece. I'll let you see your children die ahead of you...

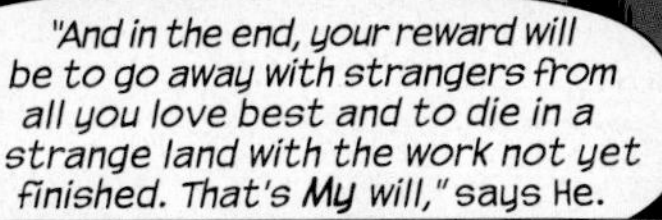
"And in the end, your reward will be to go away with strangers from all you love best and to die in a strange land with the work not yet finished. That's My will," says He.

"Thy will be done," says I, and in my heart, I curse Him and ask, "Why, why, WHY?"

Nick marveled that there could be so many tears in such an old woman, who seemed as dry and thin as a dead twig.
Help me along, Nick...
I only want to do what's right...

At one o'clock, after lunch, they packed up.

Half of them would ride in the wrecker Dick and Ralph had found in Columbus; half in the new Dodge van; a CB radio crackling between them.

As they rattled off, driving west on Route 30, Abagail Freemantle did not look back once and she did not cry.
Her crying was done.

She was set in the center of the Lord's will...and His will would be done...

Thy will be done, she thought, but she also thought of that red eye opening in the sky, and she was afraid...

1 VARIANT

COVER BY MIKE PERKINS & LAURA MARTIN

2

COVER BY LEE BERMEJO & LAURA MARTIN

2 VARIANT

COVER BY MIKE PERKINS & LAURA MARTIN

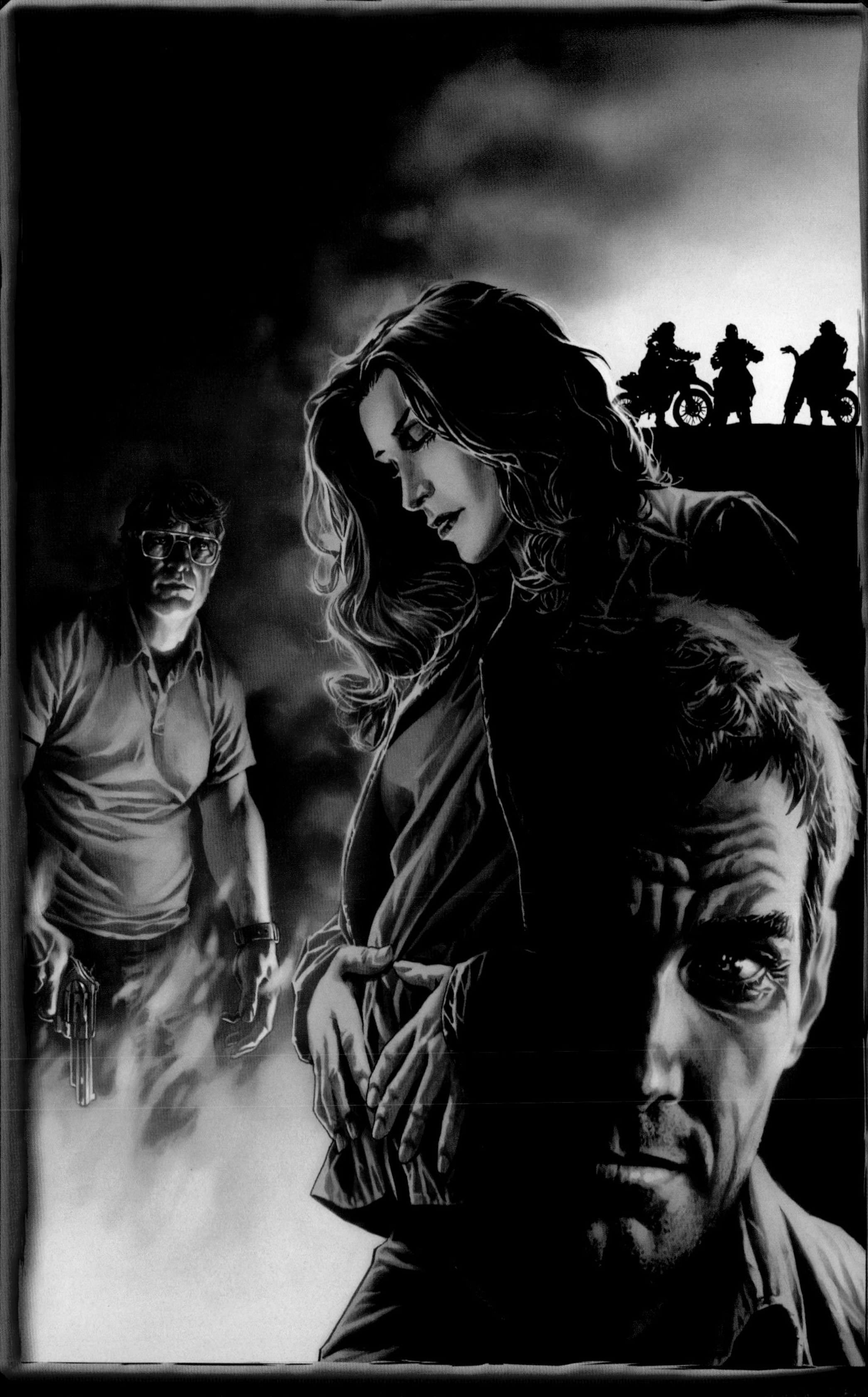

3

COVER BY LEE BERMEJO & LAURA MARTIN

4 VARIANT

COVER BY MIKE PERKINS & LAURA MARTIN

5

COVER BY LEE BERMEJO & LAURA MARTIN

5 VARIANT

COVER BY MIKE PERKINS & LAURA MARTIN

SCRIPT TO FINAL

PAGE ONE.

PANEL ONE.

A close-up or medium-shot of Fran, in her sleeping bag, writing in a spiral notebook. A flashlight by her side is illuminatin the page. (Or maybe she's holding it?) In the background, Stu, Harold, and Glen Bateman are asleep, all of them arranged aroun an extinguished campfire. (NOTE: We're going to be cutting to some version of this "journaling" scene a few times, Mike, sinc it's the convention of the issue.) NOTE TO LETTERER: Can we do something with the captions in this issue to reflect it's Fran nie's handwriting we're reading?

FLOATING TEXT: FROM FRAN GOLDSMITH'S DIARY.

CAPTION: JULY 8TH.

CAPTION: It's late, but I should try to get as much of what happened down before my eyelids just SLAM SHUT.

PANEL TWO.

Take us inside the CDC—into the room where Stu was being held captive. And where he killed his captor and would-be murdere From the ground-level, we're looking up at: Fran, who is covering her mouth in mid-gasp (on the left-hand side of the panel Glenn, in the middle, a stony expression on his face; and Harold, on the right, who looks queasy and sick. They are all lookin down at something.

CAPTION: We went into the CDC in Stovington today. Me, Harold, and Mr. Bateman, while Stu waited outside. It was spooky, let m tell you. Like a haunted house.

GLENN: I don't think we'd better say anything to Stu about this room...

(CONTINUED)

PAGE ONE (CONTINUED).

PANEL THREE.

Now we're behind our threesome and we're looking at what they're looking at, which is: The broken corpse of the man Stu kille face down in a pool of his dried blood. The smashed chair (Stu wielded) off to the corpse's side.

GLENN: ...I believe Mr. Redman came very close to dying in this room.

PANEL FOUR.

Cut to: Exterior, CDC. In the foreground, on the left-hand side of the panel, we have: Stu, sitting on a low stone wall, with hi back to the building 'cause he can't even look at it. In the middle of the panel, in the middle- or background, we have Franni and then Glenn, and then Harold, walking towards Stu through a field that is overgrown. Frannie is moving with some urgenc towards Stu, her heart going out towards him.

CAPTION: Once Harold's curiosity was satisfied, we went back out, and... I wanted to just HUG and KISS Stu.

CAPTION: I felt ashamed, diary. That we hadn't believed Stu about the plague center and that we'd all complained about wha an awful time we'd had when Captain Trips happened and he'd barely said anything.

PANEL FIVE.

Continuous. A close-up on Frannie's face/head, filling the panel. Her eyes wet with emotion.

CAPTION: That's when I realized... I was falling in love with Stu. I had the world's most CRUSHABLE CRUSH on him, and if i wasn't for Harold I'd take my damn chances...

'AGE TWO.

'ANEL ONE.

ut to our foursome sitting or standing around Stu (on that wall), variously. Listening to him as he talks.

APTION: Anyway, that was when Stu told us he wanted to go to Nebraska.

APTION: He wanted to check on this old lady he'd been dreaming about lately, he said.

TU: Her name's Mother Abagail, and she lives in a place called Holland Home or Hometown or something like that. In a field f corn.

ANEL TWO.

ut to: The chain-link fence that encircles the CDC. Harold is sitting cross-legged on the ground, painting a sign that leans gainst the fence. (That's on the left-hand side of the panel.) To his right, we have: Glenn, Frannie, and Stu, standing in a lump. Glenn has one of his hands hooked into the fence.

APTION: While Harold made his sign, we had a very sober talk about Stu's dreams. About this woman. About the bogeyman.

APTION: Dreams we'd each been having, in some shape or other.

LENN: It's remarkable...

LENN: ...but we all seem to be sharing an authentic psychic experience.

ANEL THREE.

few beats later. The sign Harold was making in the previous panel is now hanging on that chain-link fence. (And of course it's ne same sign Larry and Nadine stumbled across last issue, Mike.) The foursome are walking away from it, towards their mopeds hich we don't have to see). From left to right we have: Glenn, Harold, Stu, and then Frannie.

APTION: Once we'd settled on a plan to find Mother Abagail (I'd take her over the dark man anytime), Harold suggested we stock p on Veronal and start taking small doses.

AROLD: To disrupt these dream-cycle.

AROLD: And stop the nightmares from coming.

ONTINUED)

AGE TWO (CONTINUED).

ANEL FOUR.

ack to a version of Page One, Panel One. Fran is in her sleeping bag, but she has finished journaling and is putting her diary way, into her knapsack (which is where she keeps it, we're establishing). In the background, everyone still sleeping.

APTION: I agreed to that plan but am gonna palm my dose because I don't know what it might do to the Lone Ranger inside me.

APTION: Besides, bad as the dark man is, I like seeing Mother Abagail in my dreams. She so exudes an aura of NICENESS and INDNESS.

ANEL FIVE.

few moments later. Staying on Fran, who has now put away her notebook, flashlight, and stuff, and has rolled over on to her de, trying to get to sleep.

APTION: I understand why Stu wants to go to her. I keep thinking if we can just get to her, everything will be A-OK.

APTION: Things to Remember, diary: The Who. Kool-Aid. Converse All-Stars. *Night of the Living Dead. Brrrr!* That last one its too close to home. I quit for the night!

Lee Bermejo's black and white art for this issue's cover.

Laura Martin on coloring the cover to this issue.

Unlike most covers that are inked with solid black, Lee's covers often feature soft edges, airbrushed glows, and pencil shading. This makes my process a bit different. Instead of "flatting" the entire image (separating each shape into a single color) and working only on one layer, I'll choose the largest elements, and put each of those sections on its own layer.

This gives me a lot more flexibility to blend my colors with Lee's pencil shading. Here you can see the sky, corn, Abby and her guitar separated into four areas by color. (The line art is faded back to see the color details.) I could have separated her skin, hair, and kerchief, but I prefer to work on as few layers as possible.

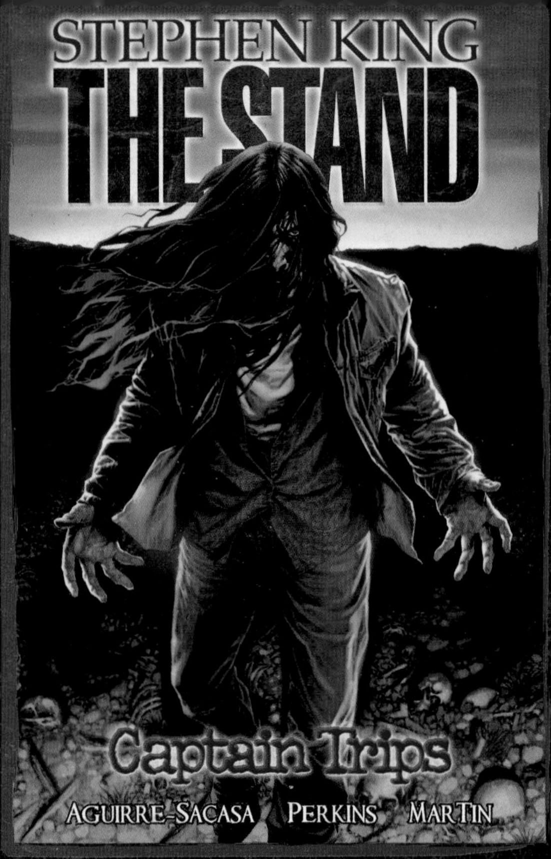

THE STORY STARTS HERE IN THESE STEPHEN KING: THE STAND COLLECTIONS

THE STAND:
CAPTAIN TRIPS
ISBN: 978-0-7851-4272-0

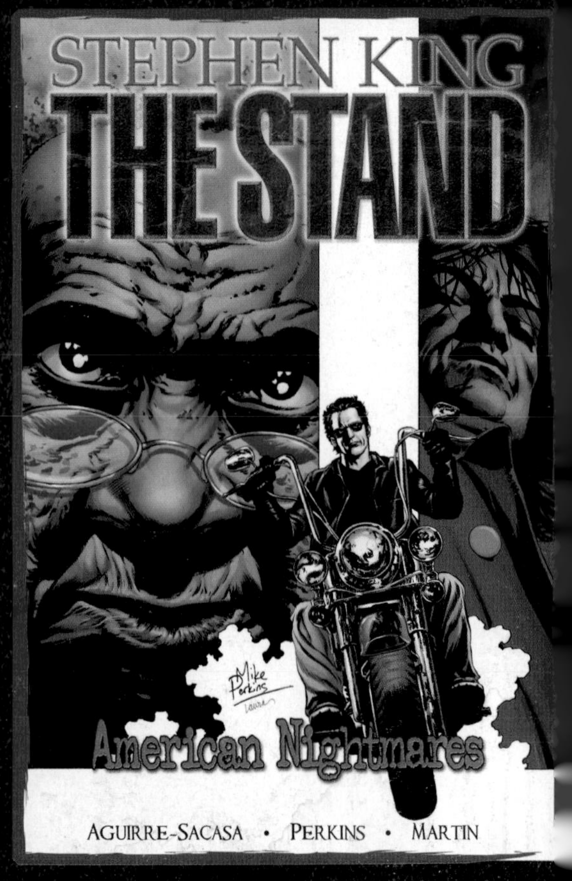

THE STAND:
AMERICAN NIGHTMARES
ISBN: 978-0-7851-4274-4